Mechanic Mike's Machines

Cars

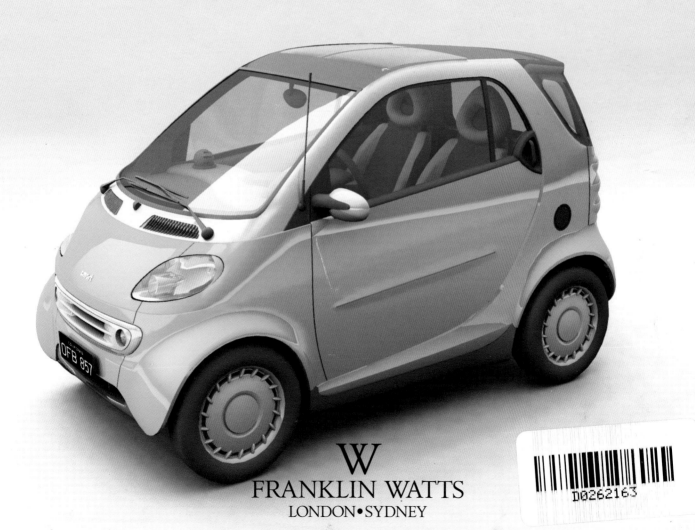

W
FRANKLIN WATTS
LONDON•SYDNEY

First published in the UK in 2014 by Franklin Watts

Franklin Watts
338 Euston Road
London NW1 3BH

Franklin Watts
Level 17/207 Kent Street
Sydney, NSW 2000

Dewey classification: 629.2'22

A CIP catalogue record for this book is available from the British Library.

ISBN: 978 1 4451 2722 4

Franklin Watts is a division of Hachette Children's Books, an Hachette UK company.
www.hachette.co.uk

MECHANIC MIKE'S MACHINES CARS
was produced for Franklin Watts by
David West Children's Books, 6 Princeton Court, 55 Felsham Road, London SW15 1AZ

Copyright © 2014 David West Children's Books

Designed and illustrated by David West

Printed in China

Mechanic Mike says:
Mike will tell you
something more about
the machine.

Find out what type
of engine drives
the car.

Discover
something you
didn't know.

Is it fast or slow?
Top speeds are
given here.

How many people
can it carry?

Get your
amazing
fact here!

Contents

Mechanic Mike says:
This Bentley was one of
the fastest sports cars
when it was built in 1929.

Supercharger

4

Vintage

Vintage cars were built between the end of World War I in 1918 and the end of 1930. This period is known as the 'vintage era'.

This car was fitted with a device on the front which super-charged the engine.

This car set a record in 1932 at Brooklands, Surrey, UK with a recorded speed of 222.03 kilometres per hour.

Did you know that Bentleys are still made today, although they look quite different?

The Bentley could carry four passengers and a driver.

This car had a 4.4 litre petrol engine with a **supercharger**.

5

Electric Car

This little town car runs on electricity. It was first designed as a petrol-engined car. Small electric cars are ideal for driving around in towns, where there are recharging stations.

This car has a 55 kW electric engine.

Did you know electric cars often do not have to pay city centre **congestion charges**?

The Smart Fortwo electric drive can carry two people.

These little cars are quick, but not fast, with a top speed of 120 kilometres per hour.

This electric car can travel 140 kilometres before the battery needs recharging.

Mechanic Mike says:
Electric cars are more friendly to the environment as they do not produce any exhaust fumes.

Mechanic Mike says:
MPVs are also called people carriers
or people movers.

MPV

These multi-purpose vehicles are popular with large families and many taxi services. Sliding passenger doors make it easier for people to get in and out.

Sliding passenger door

 These cars are often fitted with a rear view camera to help the driver see what's behind.

 MPVs can be quite speedy with a top speed of more than 210 kilometres per hour.

 MPVs can usually carry about eight people.

 Did you know the first MPV looked like a silver teardrop? It was made in 1913.

 MPVs are powered by either petrol or diesel engines.

Mini Van

Mini vans are just like cars, except that the back half has no windows. These vehicles are used by all types of workers who want to carry goods or tools in the back, instead of passengers.

Mini vans are popular vehicles for airbrush artists to work on.

These small vans have a top speed of 145 kilometres per hour.

These vans can only carry two people.

They use either diesel or petrol engines. Some have electric motors instead.

Did you know that mini vans are so popular that all big European car makers sell them?

11

Mechanic Mike says:
Some countries have their own word for pick-up, such as ute in Australia and New Zealand, or bakkie in South Africa.

Pickup

Pickups are similar to saloon cars but they also have an open cargo area over the back wheels. The cabin area can seat either two or five people.

An ute, short for 'utility' or 'coupé utility', is a term used in Australia and New Zealand to describe passenger vehicles with a cargo area at the back.

High performance versions of these cars can reach 271 kilometres per hour.

Pickups can seat either two or five people, depending on the size of the cabin.

Did you know that the ute was the result of a 1932 letter from a farmer's wife in Australia to the Ford Motor Company, asking for 'a vehicle to go to church in on Sundays, and which can carry our pigs to market on Mondays'?

These cars can be powered by either petrol or diesel engines.

Mechanic Mike says:
The first Jeeps were made for the US army during World War II.

4x4

Vehicles with four wheels that have power to all four wheels are called 4x4s. Rugged cars, such as Jeeps, can be driven off-road over rough ground.

These cars have large tyres for extra grip off-road.

Did you know that US soldiers gave the Jeep its name after Eugene the Jeep, a cartoon character that could go anywhere?

4x4s can travel over 160 kilometres per hour. These cars are not built for speed.

Jeeps can carry four people and a driver.

These cars are powered by diesel or petrol engines.

Sports Car

Sports cars like this Pontiac are small and fast. They **accelerate** very quickly, going from 0 to 96.6 kilometres per hour in 5 seconds!

Mechanic Mike says:
Some cars like this one have **turbochargers**, which boost the power of the engine.

16

Sports cars have two doors, usually two seats and are very lightweight.

Did you know the first sports car was built in 1910?

This sports car has a top speed of 229 kilometres per hour.

Sports cars like this one can only carry two people.

This car has a four cylinder petrol engine.

Supercar

Supercars are fast, sporty and expensive. This Bugatti Veyron is one of the fastest road cars in the world.

Mechanic Mike says:
When the Bugatti Veyron Sport came out it cost about £1.7 million.

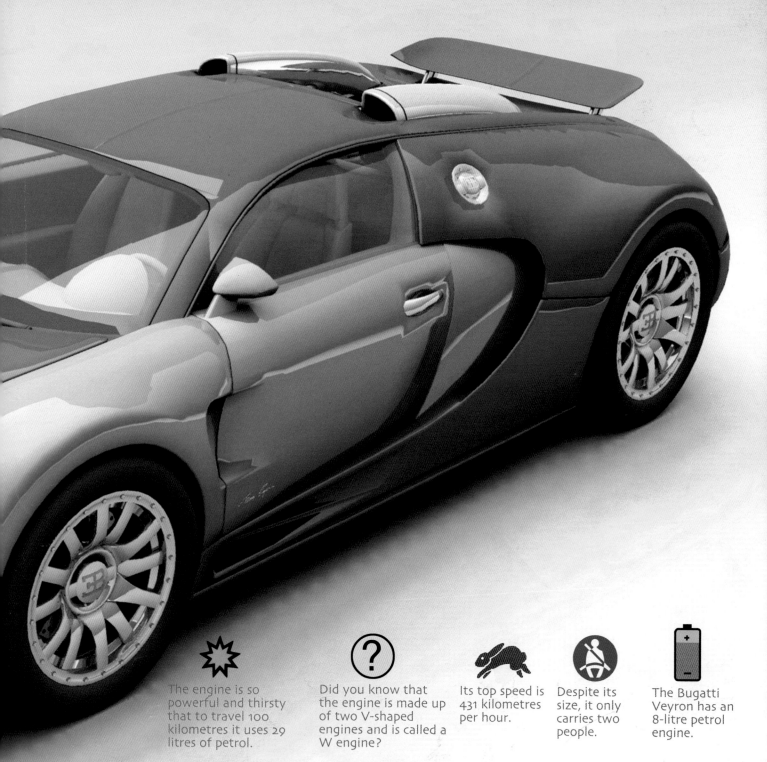

The engine is so powerful and thirsty that to travel 100 kilometres it uses 29 litres of petrol.

Did you know that the engine is made up of two V-shaped engines and is called a W engine?

Its top speed is 431 kilometres per hour.

Despite its size, it only carries two people.

The Bugatti Veyron has an 8-litre petrol engine.

Police Car

This Dodge Charger police car is a powerful machine used by many police forces. It is fitted with sirens and red and blue warning lights.

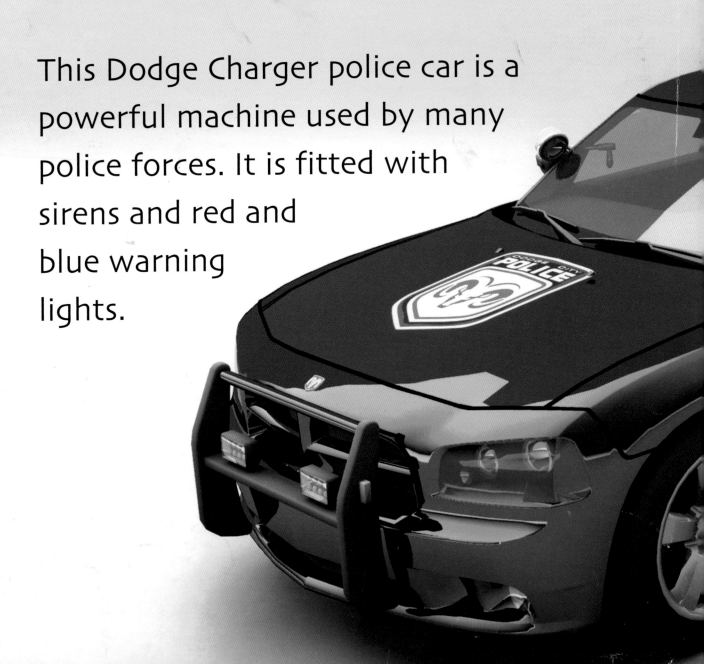

Patrolling police cars are sometimes called **panda cars**. Others are IRVs, 'immediate response vehicles'.

Did you know the first police car was an electric wagon used in the USA in 1899?

Police pursuit vehicles (PPVs) can reach 241 kilometres per hour.

Police cars are similar to family saloons, which can seat five. Most police cars have a driver and one other officer.

This police car has a 5.7 litre, V8 petrol engine.

Mechanic Mike says:
Police cars are usually called squad cars or patrol cars.

Hot Rod

Hot rods are a type of **customised** car. They are usually American cars with large engines that have been altered to go fast.

Mechanic Mike says:
It's not just the engine, but all the parts of a hot rod that are modified. This includes suspension, the interior and even the shape of the body.

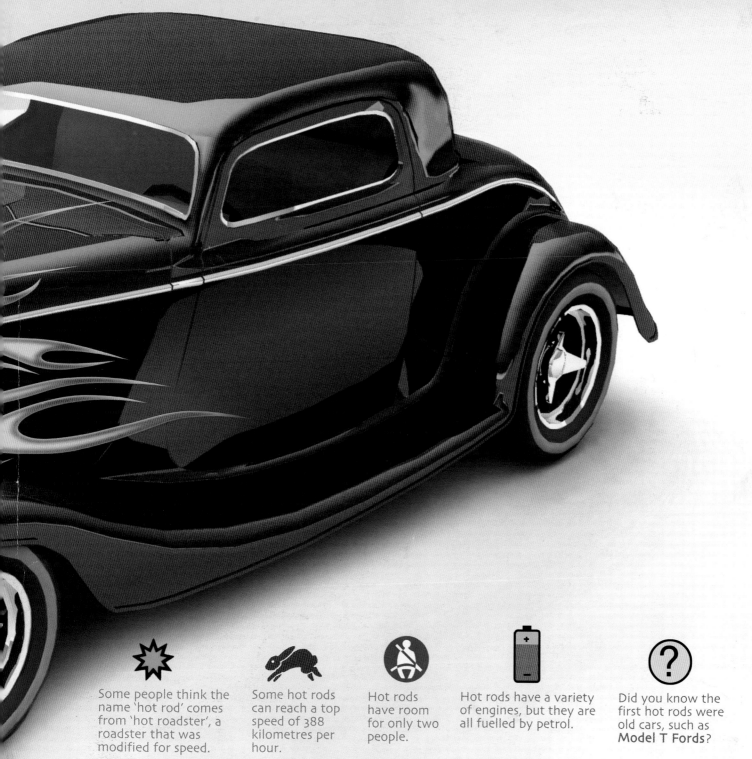

Some people think the name 'hot rod' comes from 'hot roadster', a roadster that was modified for speed.

Some hot rods can reach a top speed of 388 kilometres per hour.

Hot rods have room for only two people.

Hot rods have a variety of engines, but they are all fuelled by petrol.

Did you know the first hot rods were old cars, such as **Model T Fords**?

23

Glossary

accelerate
Increase in speed.

congestion charge
Fees motorists pay to enter a city centre, charged to keep traffic levels down.

customised
Changed to be exactly as a person wants it.

Model T Ford
The first affordable car, built by the Ford Motor Company in 1908.

panda cars
Small to medium-sized police patrol cars. So called because their black and white markings resembled those of a panda.

Police Pursuit Vehicles
US police cars that are fast enough for pursuit and for high-speed response calls.

supercharger
A mechanical device fitted to an engine to make it more powerful.

turbocharger
Similar to a supercharger.

Index